BASIC PRINCIPLES OF LEADERSHIP:

Insights on Developing Trust Through Servant Leadership

Clarence D. Davis

Copyright © by Clarence D. Davis 2022. All
rights reserved.
Before this document is duplicated or
reproduced in any manner, the publisher's
consent must be gained. Therefore, the contents within can neither be stored electronically, transferred, nor kept in a database. Neither in Part nor full can the
document be copied.

Table of Contents

INTRODUCTION 5

PART ONE 7

Extraordinary authority includes serving others. 7

PART TWO 10

Provide your staff with a dream representing things to come. 10

PART THREE 13

The best chiefs upset the conventional order. .. 13

PART FOUR 15

Fruitful pioneers use a lot of commendation. ... 15

PART FIVE 18

Here and there, a divert is superior to a censure. 18

PART SIX 20

Change your initiative style as indicated by your colleagues' ability and responsibility. 20

PART SEVEN 23

Your representatives are your clients, as well!.23

PART EIGHT 26

Your staff needs limits to unreservedly work...26

PART NINE 29

A believed pioneer is a convincing pioneer. 29

PART TEN 31

Your kin ought not to fear you. 31

PART ELEVEN 35

The best chiefs focus on honesty...................... 35

PART TWELVE 38

A sign of incredible initiative is having the option to apologize. 38

CONCLUSION 40

The vital message in these books is that:.......... 40

INTRODUCTION

How might this benefit me? Find the basic insights that shape each extraordinary pioneer.

It's a verifiable truth: associations are just basically as great as individuals who lead them. Without extraordinary initiative, an organization and its staff can't arrive at their maximum capacity. It's simply impractical.

However, what is the incredible initiative?

It might sound illogical, however, is an incredible pioneer really includes .

. . being a worker! Worker initiative is an approach to driving that puts your representatives and clients first, and you second. It's anything but simple expertise to grow, yet it can immensely affect how successful you are as chief - and the consequences for your group.

In these books to basic principles of leadership, you'll find the presence of mind authority tips that have a major effect. In spite of the fact that we can't cover every one of the bits of insight, we've carefully selected our thought processes are the most valuable important points.

PART ONE

Extraordinary authority includes serving others.

To sort out what kind of pioneer you need to be, you really want to do something straightforward: pay attention to your heart. What does it say? Does it murmur that you ought to serve the benefit of everyone? Or on the other hand, does it let you know that you ought to follow your own restricted personal circumstance and not care about who gets injured en route?

When you comprehend your internal inspiration, you'll know whether you need to be a terrible pioneer - or a worker chief.

As a worker chief, your need is to serve your subordinates and your more extensive association as opposed to yourself. By and by, that implies providing your kin with a solid internal compass. A worker chief's group ought to see precisely the exact thing results they're pursuing - and what achievement resembles.

Up until this point, this could seem like pretty standard administration conduct. Be that as it may, the worker chief accomplishes something different, as well. Whenever you've given your kin a few objectives, you assist your subordinates with accomplishing these objectives. You serve your staff by offering input and preparing amazing open doors. You likewise carve out the opportunity to tune in and figure out what support they need.

By giving vital bearing and a ton of everyday help, you'll appreciate incredible outcomes and extraordinary working associations with your kin.

PART TWO

Provide your staff with a dream representing things to come.

Do you have a dream for your organization's future? To be an extraordinary worker pioneer, you'll have to make one - and share it with your staff to move and persuade them toward a shared objective. It isn't muddled to Create a dream. Be that as it may, it includes addressing three unavoidable issues.

The main inquiry is, What's the general motivation behind your organization? At the end of the day, what sort of business would you say you are ready? To track down your response, attempt to dive as deep as could really be expected. Take, for instance, Disney. Disney's vision isn't to be a diversion organization; rather they depict themselves as being "occupied with joy."

The subsequent inquiry is, What does achievement seem to be in your organization? All things considered, when your kin understand what they're going for the gold, is ready to arrive quicker. Disney is extremely clear about what achievement resembles: blesses clients' countenances from the moment they enter their amusement parks to the second they leave once more.

The third inquiry is, What are your organization's values? These qualities will direct your firm along the way to progress - so you should get them right. Disney's main worth is security, trailed by the graciousness and guaranteeing that each staff part puts on an extraordinary act for their amusement park guests.

Whenever you've arranged the responses to these inquiries, you'll have made a rousing vision to impart to your kin.

PART THREE

The best chiefs upset the conventional order.

Who's at the head of the established pecking order in your business? For most organizations, it's the chief. What's more, the occupation of everybody underneath the pioneer is to be receptive to their needs and needs.

In any case, this sort of arrangement is an error. Why? Since pioneers ought not to be at the highest point of the pyramid. The best position has a place with another person: your client.

The best organizations spin around what the client needs - not the huge chief. Everybody in your organization, regardless of how senior, ought to attempt to take special care of the necessities of your clients. They ought to likewise really focus on individuals dealing with the cutting edge who truly communicate with clients consistently. Incredible pioneers realize that standing by listening to their bleeding edge staff is the best way to comprehend their clients genuinely.

In addition to the fact that extraordinary pioneers pay attention to their workers, they likewise urge them to concoct their own thoughts.

This is one more approach to upsetting the customary initiative-ordered progression. So rather than providing hierarchical orders, cultivate a climate where everybody helps set the plan. Thus, the obligation will stream down the levels of leadership, and each staff part will turn into a forerunner by their own doing.

PART FOUR

Fruitful pioneers use a lot of commendation.

Terrible pioneers are a great deal like seagulls - when their partners aren't gaining sufficient headway toward their objectives, they dive in, make a clamor, dump in their group, and afterward take off.

Fortunately, making the progress from a seagull to an incredible pioneer is simpler than you could suspect. Everything boils down to a distinct advantage: acclaim.

Rather than showing up when things turn out badly, the best chiefs show up when something goes right. As opposed to searching because of motivations to reprimand, great pioneers are continuously looking for something to laud their workers for. That's what they know, by applauding appropriate conduct, they're making it almost certain that the individual will rehash this conduct from now on.

Yet, how would you offer commendation actually? To start with, be explicit. When you see somebody who's performing great, approach them and tell them precisely the thing they're doing well. Ensure they know how thankful you are, and make sense of why their heavenly exhibition matters to such an extent. At last, urge them to continue doing what they're doing, and let them in that you have a ton of trust in them. Wrap up the discussion by ensuring your associate realizes that you appreciate - and will keep on supporting - them.

PART FIVE

Here and there, a divert is superior to a censure.

As you're likely mindful, people commit errors. Also, your staff is no special case! As a pioneer, it's your obligation to focus when errors are made - and to ensure similar slip-ups don't reoccur.

How you respond when a representative commits an error ought to rely on how experienced they are. On the off chance that somebody's failing to meet expectations yet has the right stuff to improve, a short censure is altogether. At the point when you censure the individual, ensure you condemn their way of behaving as opposed to them personally.

In any case, how would it be advisable for you to respond when somebody performs inadequately and doesn't have any idea how to do any better? All things considered, in a quickly impacting world, all of us are continually learning. Also, censuring students is absurd - or useful. At the point when students commit errors, it's your occupation as a pioneer to divert instead of censuring them.

You can do this by going through their exhibition bit by bit and checking on what turned out badly.

During this audit, ensure your partner sees precisely the exact thing their objective is and the way that they can more readily make progress toward it later on. At last, let the individual in on that this one slip-up doesn't characterize them - that you actually have a lot of trust in them to get it right sometime later.

PART SIX

Change your initiative style as indicated by your colleagues' ability and responsibility.

When a pioneer has fostered their own style of initiative, they generally stick to it. As a matter of fact, a big part of all pioneers never changes their initiative style. Yet, the best chiefs realize that adaptability is significant; to obtain ideal outcomes, they lead different colleagues in various ways.

Rather than having a one-size-fits-all methodology, check out the profile of every one of your subordinates prior to choosing how to lead them. In particular, ask yourself how capable the individual is - and that they are so dedicated to their work. Then lead in like manner.

For example, an exciting fledgling is somebody with a low degree of capability but a serious level of responsibility. Excited amateurs need clear and direct initiative, and to have somebody intently watching what they are doing.

Then again, a baffled student is to some degree skilled but has a low degree of responsibility. This individual could do with an instructing style of an initiative to work on their exhibition.

At last, you might be sufficiently fortunate to have an independent achiever in your group. This individual joins an elevated degree of capability with similarly high responsibility. Independent achievers in all actuality do best with pioneers who essentially delegate assignments and allow them to continue ahead with their work.

PART SEVEN

Your representatives are your clients, as well!

Most pioneers comprehend that their organization's clients ought to be their main concern. However, incredible pioneers realize that the main clients sit inside - not outside - their association. That is on the grounds that they consider everyone who works for them to be a client, as well.

This could sound unusual, however, when you consider it, it seems OK. All things considered, clients are so valuable since they make benefit your business. In any case, isn't that precisely what your staff individuals do, as well? It's just because of their abilities in regions like deals, showcasing, item improvement, and client care that you even have outer clients. Subsequently, your staff is really your most significant client; their persistent effort drives your main concern.

In view of this, pioneers ought to zero in on enabling, creating, and paying attention to their kin - and establishing a climate where their requirements are focused. It could feel awkward to zero in additional on your workers than your clients, yet recall that this approach will prompt more prominent consumer loyalty, not less. At the point when your staff are cheerful and feel upheld to take care of their responsibilities in the most ideal manner, then, at that point, your business will go from one solidarity to another. Eventually, that will help your clients by giving them better assistance and better items.

PART EIGHT

Your staff needs limits to unreservedly work.

A few chiefs imagine that engaging their kin implies giving them the opportunity to do anything they desire. In any case, extraordinary pioneers know that the most ideal way to make their kin independent . . . is to give them limits.

Not persuaded?

Think about a quick streaming waterway. Without stream banks on one or the other side of it, this strong waterway would immediately turn into a major puddle. However, with limits set up, the water is directed to make a strong power. Your group is a great deal like the waterway; they need limits to keep them streaming in the correct heading.

How might you set up these limits? As a rule, it's pretty much as simple as ensuring your representatives have the right data. For example, your kin ought to be sure about their objectives - as well as your assumptions for their exhibition and what guidelines they ought to meet. They ought to likewise have decent working information on every one of the standards and guidelines that oversee your industry.

At long last, your staff ought to constantly depend on the speed of your organization's arrangements and methodology. Set up, these arrangements, rules, and assumptions structure the limits your representatives will work inside. They probably won't sound energizing, yet they are the waterway banks that divert your kin's energy in the correct course.

PART NINE

A believed pioneer is a convincing pioneer.

Trust is a fundamental piece of administration. At the point when your kin trust you, they'll be more imaginative, work all the more productively and appreciate better degrees of resolve. Then again, on the off chance that you're seen as conniving, your group will meet you with obstruction, lower efficiency, and separation.

In any case, what characteristics does a believed pioneer exemplify? Most importantly, they're capable.

Everybody in the group accepts that the pioneer knows how to go about their business. Second, they have uprightness. At the point when they say they will follow through with something, their kin realizes that they're really going to make it happen. To wrap things up, they're warm. These pioneers can be relied upon to encourage their representatives. In addition to the fact that they are amicable, they exhibit genuine consideration and worry for their kin's prosperity.

There's an extraordinary method for figuring out how much your partners trust you: ask them! It could feel overwhelming, yet don't hesitate for even a moment to request input about your capability levels, your uprightness, and your relational abilities. Not exclusively will you get significant data you can follow up on, yet you'll likewise exhibit weakness by freeing yourself up to analysis along these lines. This is significant; allowing yourself to be a smidgen weak around your group is an indispensable piece of worker initiative.

PART TEN

Your kin ought not to fear you.

A few chiefs treat dread as an initiative procedure; they accept that individuals turn out more diligently for pioneers they're somewhat terrified of. These are the pioneers who yell at individuals, condemn them, and feature every single misstep they make. Yet, incredible pioneers realize that ingraining dread doesn't obtain great outcomes. It's the inverse, as a matter of fact. At the point when individuals fear their chief, they perform worse. All things considered, they essentially work harder to conceal their slip-ups. They additionally abstain from taking on enormous, testing objectives since they realize that disappointment won't go on without serious consequences.

Then again, extraordinary pioneers endeavor to limit or dispose of any apprehension their workers could feel toward them. Be that as it may, how?

Indeed, the main thing they do is act reliably. Your staff will be significantly less terrified of you in the event that they can without hesitation foresee how you're probably going to act in specific circumstances. On the off chance that you show backing to another representative who's had a go at a novel, new thing yet hasn't exactly made it work, different representatives might feel upheld assuming they take a stab at something a piece strong.

Second, rather than shouting and scrutinizing when individuals commit errors, great pioneers transform these mix-ups into workable minutes - and they give instruction on the most proficient method to improve sometime later.

At last, the best chiefs limit dread by basically being affable. Saying please and thank you doesn't cost anything, and it goes quite far to building a decent connection with your representatives.

PART ELEVEN

The best chiefs focus on honesty.

Extraordinary pioneers all share one quality practically speaking: honesty. The word uprightness begins from Latin and, generally interpreted, implies entire or not divided. At the point when you have uprightness, your entire self is adjusted, and your words match your activities. At the point when you act without respectability - when you talk the discussion yet don't walk the walk - the trust disintegrates among you and your workers. Why? Since they can never again believe a word you say.

You can act with more noteworthy honesty by remaining consistent with the Five P's of Ethical Leadership. The main P represents reason; genuinely trustworthy pioneers utilize their general reason to drive their everyday way of behaving. The subsequent P represents pride; as opposed to being narcissistic, great pioneers have a solid deep satisfaction that is situated in fearlessness. This fearlessness comes from knowing that they're able. The third P represents tolerance; that's what trustworthy pioneers trust, as long as they adhere to their directing qualities, everything will ultimately pan out. The fourth P represents diligence; each great chief has the coarseness to finish what has been started when circumstances become difficult, and they stay faithful to their standards. The last P represents viewpoint; pioneers with uprightness not just keep their entire selves in the arrangement - they keep their activities lined up with their organization's greater picture, as well.

PART TWELVE

A sign of incredible initiative is having the option to apologize.

It's miserable yet obvious: at some point, we as a whole break somebody's trust. Albeit this break can feel irreversible, there's really something straightforward you can do to get a relationship in the groove again. You can apologize. That being said, there's a craftsmanship to making a compelling conciliatory sentiment; if you need to reestablish the relationship, you need to express sorry in the correct manner.

While making a statement of regret, begin by assuming a sense of ownership with what you've done. Try not to attempt to pardon it or utilize contingent words like "if" and "however." These words suggest that you're moving the fault. Second, make it clear to the individual that you comprehend the aggravation you've caused them; don't attempt to limit this aggravation to cheer yourself up. Give the individual space to enlighten you regarding this aggravation, as well. Stand by listening to the effect that your activities have had on them. At long last, make certain to end your expression of remorse by focusing on not rehashing anything that you've done. Keep in mind, that your conciliatory sentiment is just worth something on the off chance that you don't copy the trust-breaking conduct.

CONCLUSION

The vital message in these books is that:

The best chiefs place trust in their representatives and work to assemble warm, steady associations with them. Instead of setting themselves at the focal point of the organization's tasks, incredible pioneers put the emphasis on their clients - and their staff.

Furthermore, here's some more significant guidance:

Data is important; share it openly.

As a pioneer, setting trust in your people is crucial. One of the most outstanding ways of showing this trust is to impart data to your representatives openly. In the event that you crowd data and keep your staff in obscurity, things can rapidly disentangle. To fill the holes in their insight, your staff will begin to make presumptions and make their own tales about what's happening. These accounts may be negative and harmful to the spirit. So have a strategy of giving out data, talking transparently, and being as legitimate as possible!

www.ingramcontent.com/pod-product-compliance
Lightning Source LLC
Chambersburg PA
CBHW050318220526
45465CB00005B/2034